SANTA SWINGS

— PIANO LEVEL —
EARLY INTERMEDIATE
(HLSPL LEVEL 4-5)

ISBN 978-1-4234-9551-2

HAL•LEONARD®
CORPORATION
7777 W. BLUEMOUND RD. P.O. BOX 13819 MILWAUKEE, WI 53213

Visit Hal Leonard Online at
www.halleonard.com

Visit Phillip at
www.phillipkeveren.com

PREFACE

Whether it's Ol' Blue Eyes belting out "The Christmas Waltz" or Nat King Cole crooning over chestnuts, Christmas and jazz just seem to go together. Wouldn't Charlie Brown's Christmas seem rather stark without Vince Guaraldi's swinging jazz piano?

All of the selections in this collection were arranged to take full advantage of jazz rhythms and harmonic colors. When in doubt, swing the eighth note and embrace the accidental!

My most sincere wishes for a Merry Christmas and a Jazzy New Year!

Phillip Keveren

BIOGRAPHY

Phillip Keveren, a multi-talented keyboard artist and composer, has composed original works in a variety of genres from piano solo to symphonic orchestra. Mr. Keveren gives frequent concerts and workshops for teachers and their students in the United States, Canada, Europe, and Asia. Mr. Keveren holds a B.M. in composition from California State University Northridge and a M.M. in composition from the University of Southern California.

CONTENTS

4   **ANGELS WE HAVE HEARD ON HIGH**

8   **THE CHRISTMAS SONG
(CHESTNUTS ROASTING ON AN OPEN FIRE)**

12   **CHRISTMAS TIME IS HERE**

18   **THE CHRISTMAS WALTZ**

15   **FROSTY THE SNOW MAN**

22   **I'LL BE HOME FOR CHRISTMAS**

28   **JINGLE BELLS**

32   **LET IT SNOW! LET IT SNOW! LET IT SNOW!**

36   **THE MOST WONDERFUL TIME OF THE YEAR**

25   **RUDOLPH THE RED-NOSED REINDEER**

40   **SANTA CLAUS IS COMIN' TO TOWN**

43   **SILVER BELLS**

48   **SKATING**

60   **SNOWFALL**

52   **UP ON THE HOUSETOP**

56   **WE WISH YOU A MERRY CHRISTMAS**

ANGELS WE HAVE HEARD ON HIGH

Traditional French Carol
Translated by JAMES CHADWICK
Arranged by Phillip Keveren

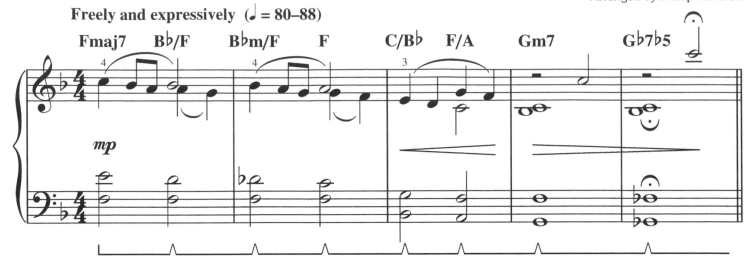

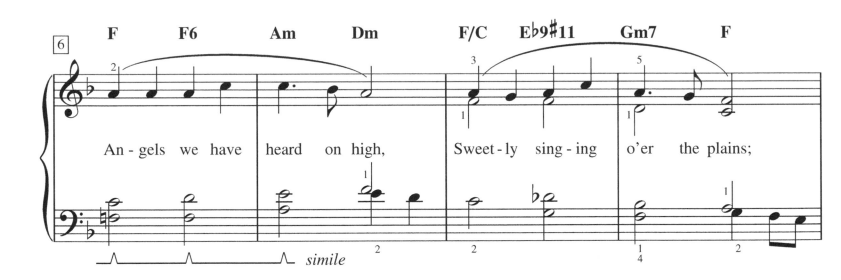

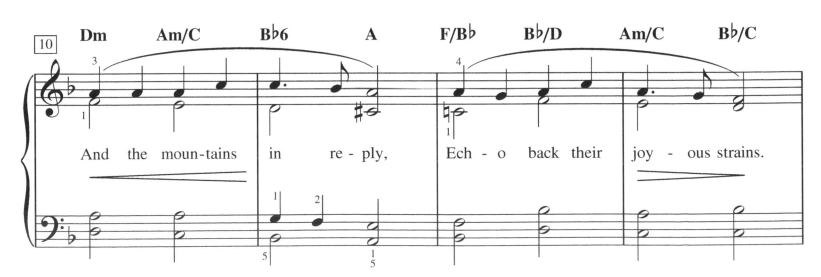

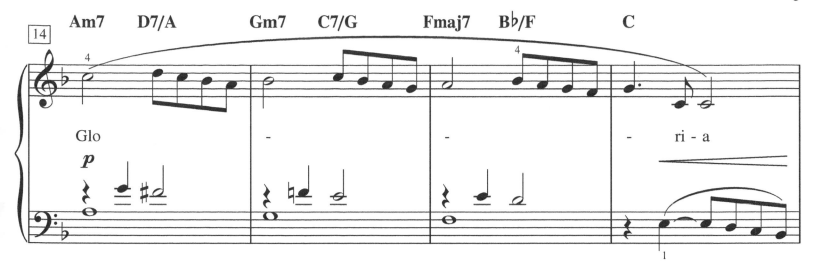

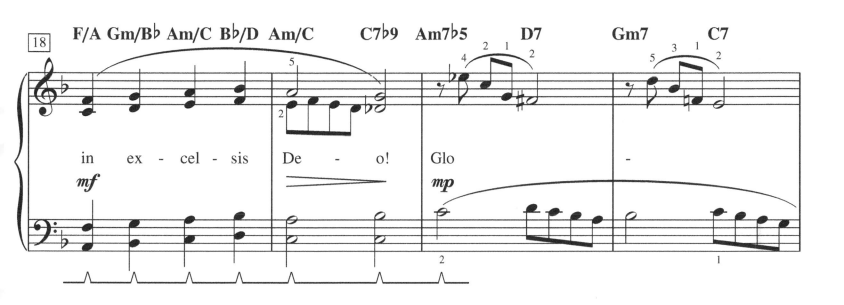

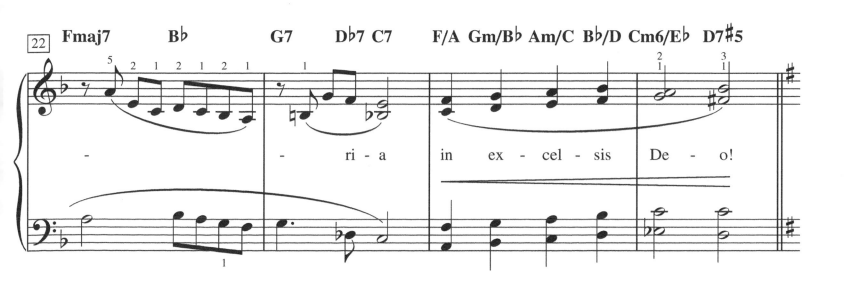

6

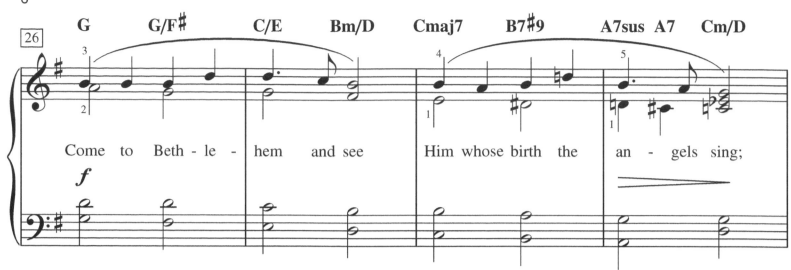

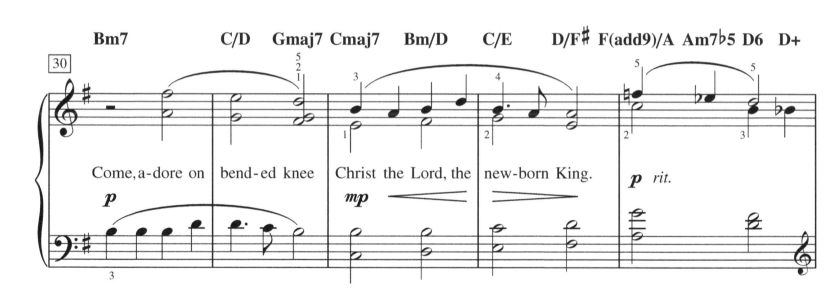

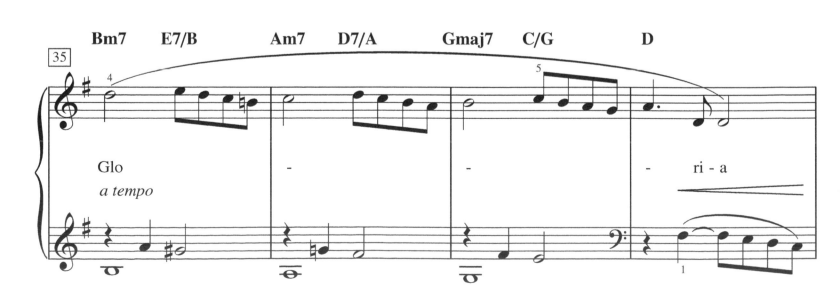

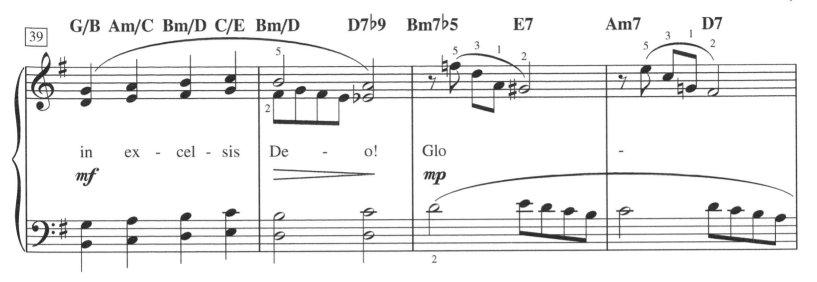

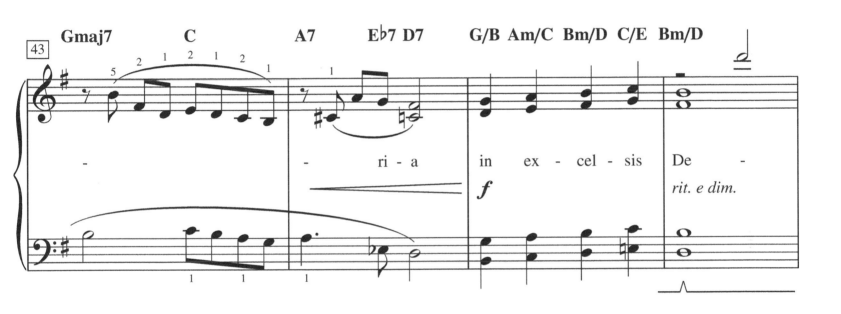

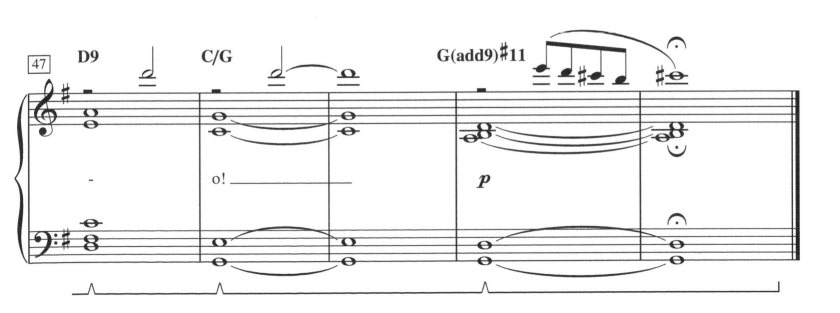

THE CHRISTMAS SONG
(Chestnuts Roasting on an Open Fire)

Music and Lyric by MEL TORME
and ROBERT WELLS
Arranged by Phillip Keveren

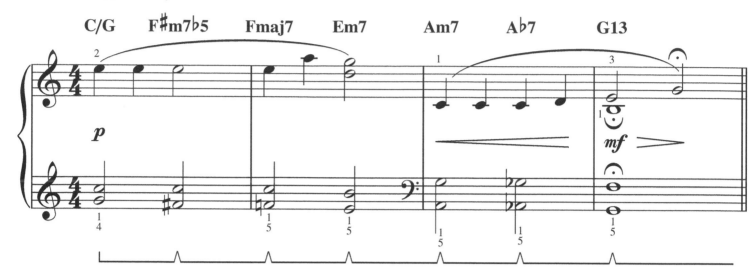

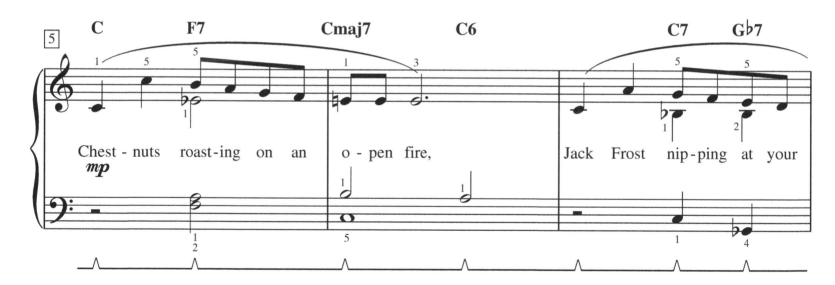

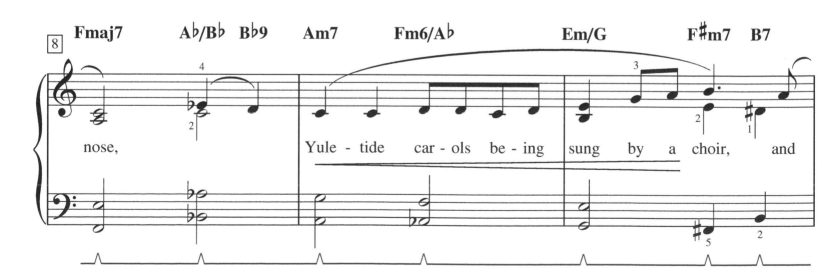

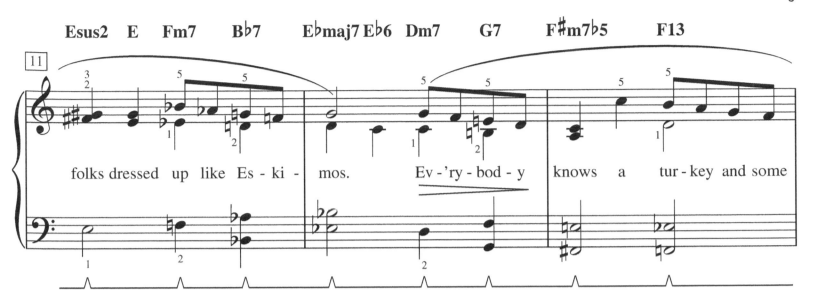

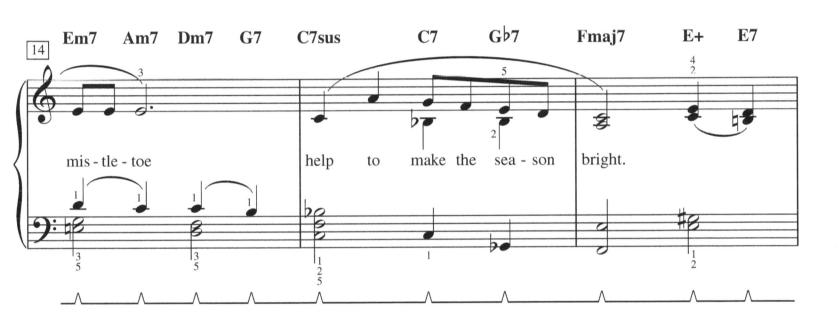

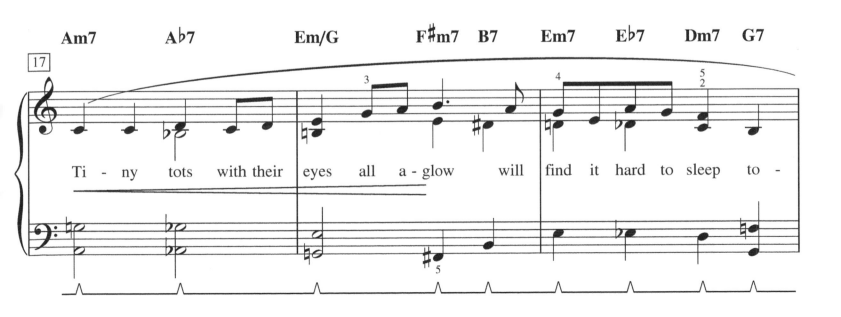

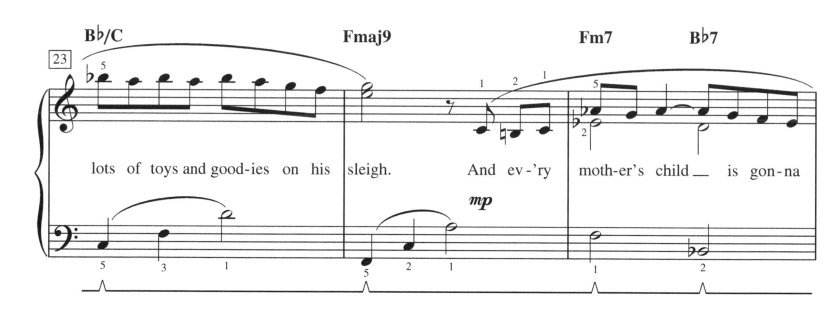

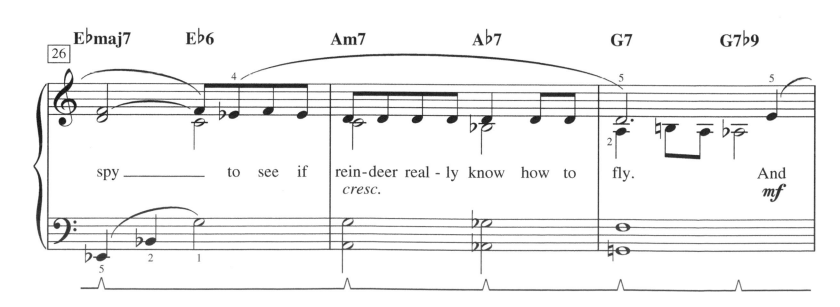

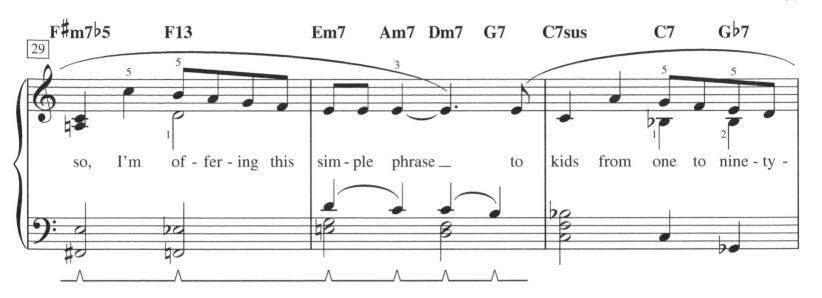

so, I'm of-fer-ing this sim-ple phrase ___ to kids from one to nine-ty-

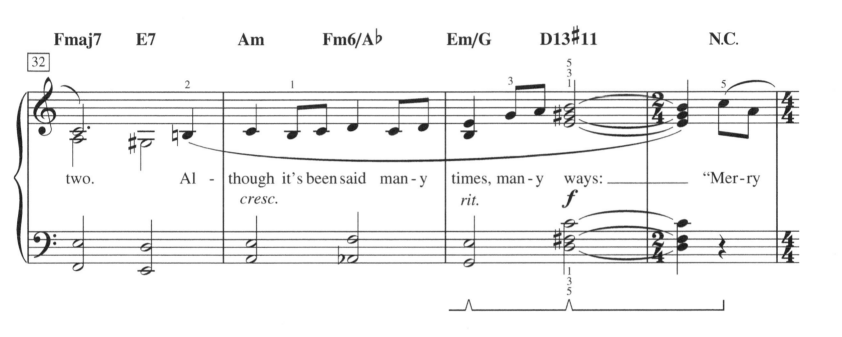

two. Al - though it's been said man-y times, man-y ways: ___ "Mer-ry

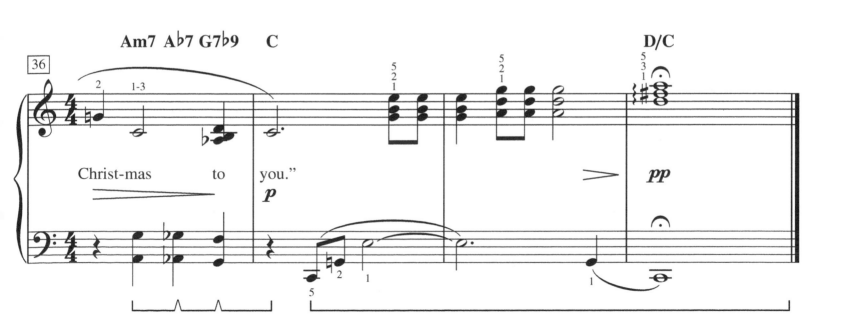

Christ-mas to you."

CHRISTMAS TIME IS HERE

from A CHARLIE BROWN CHRISTMAS™

Words by LEE MENDELSON
Music by VINCE GUARALDI
Arranged by Phillip Keveren

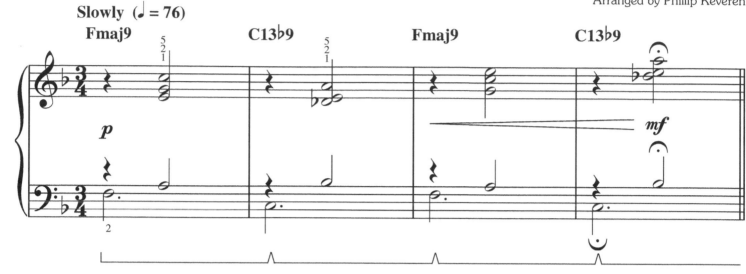

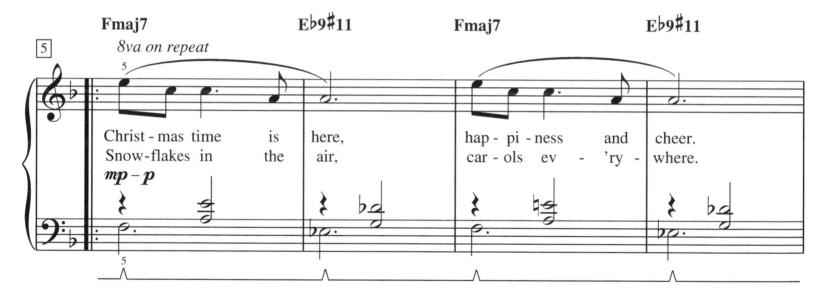

Christ - mas time   is   here,   hap - pi - ness   and   cheer.
Snow - flakes in   the   air,   car - ols ev - 'ry - where.

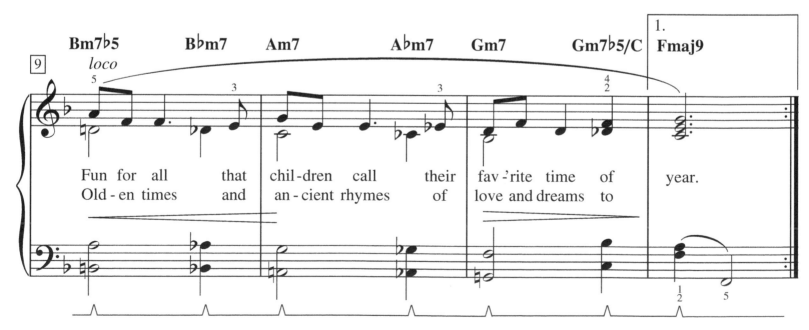

Fun for all   that   chil - dren call   their   fav - 'rite time of   year.
Old - en times and   an - cient rhymes of   love and dreams to

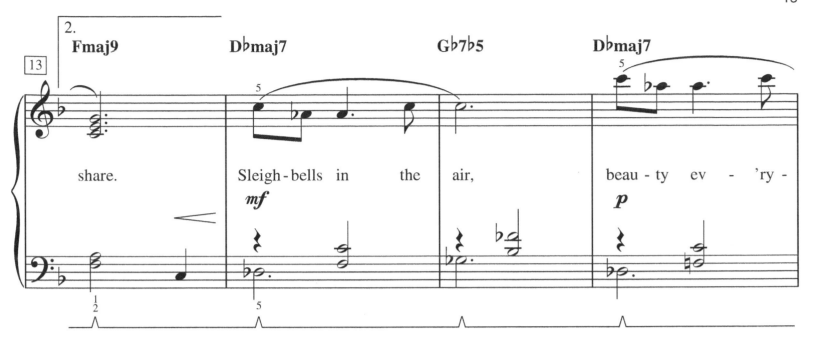

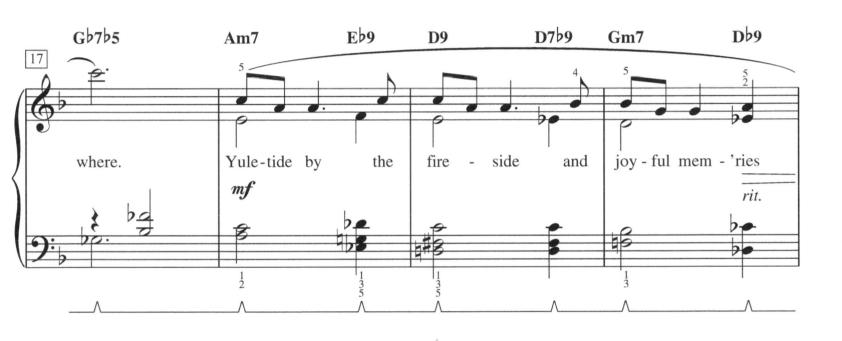

14

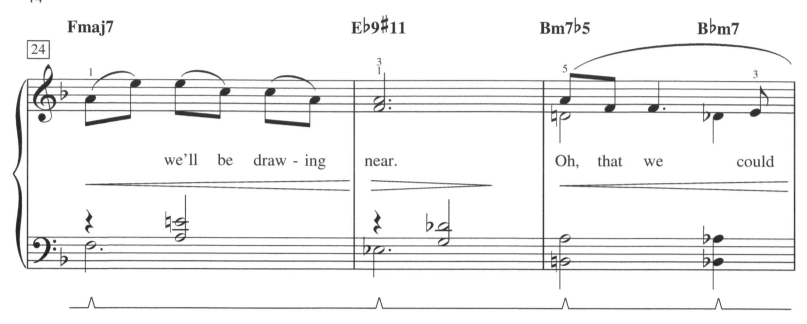

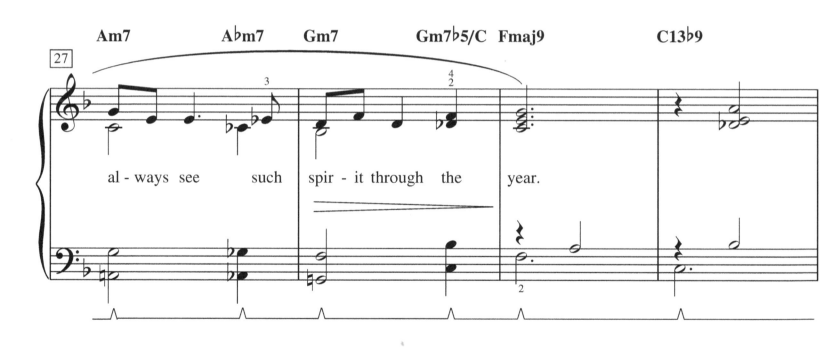

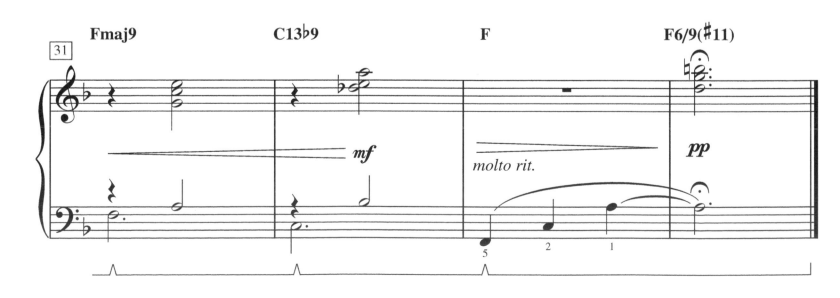

FROSTY THE SNOW MAN

Words and Music by STEVE NELSON
and JACK ROLLINS
Arranged by Phillip Keveren

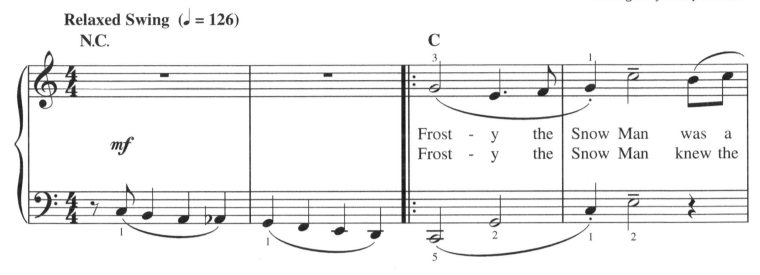

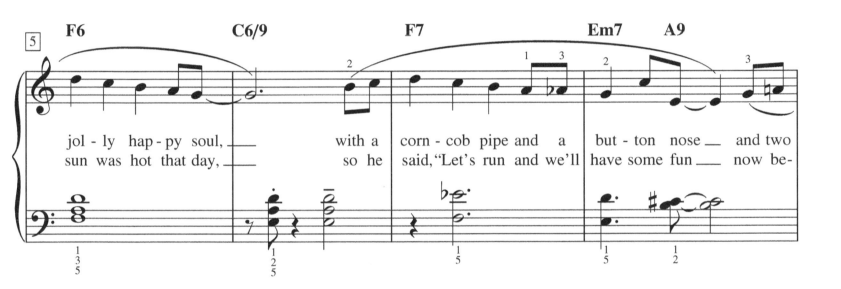

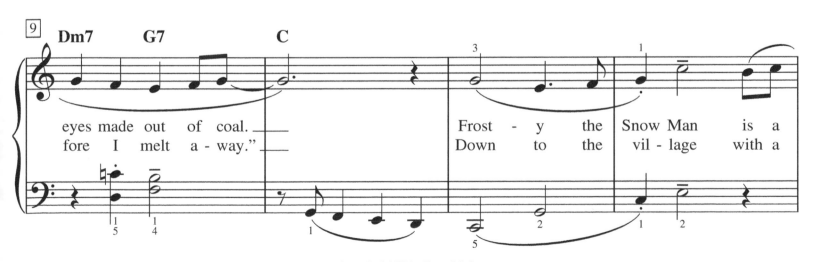

17

THE CHRISTMAS WALTZ

Words by SAMMY CAHN
Music by JULE STYNE
Arranged by Phillip Keveren

Sentimentally (♩ = 126–132)

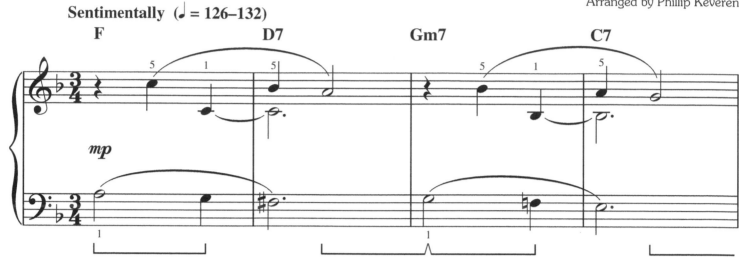

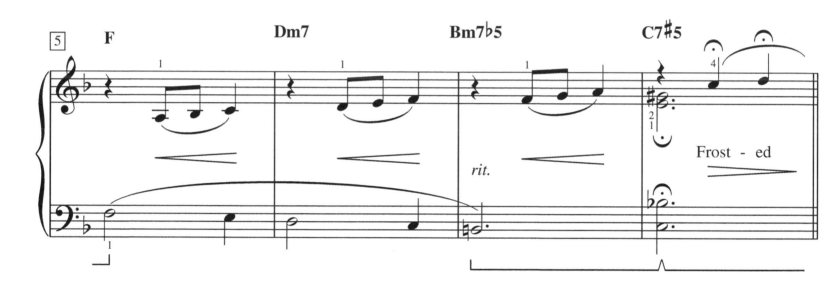

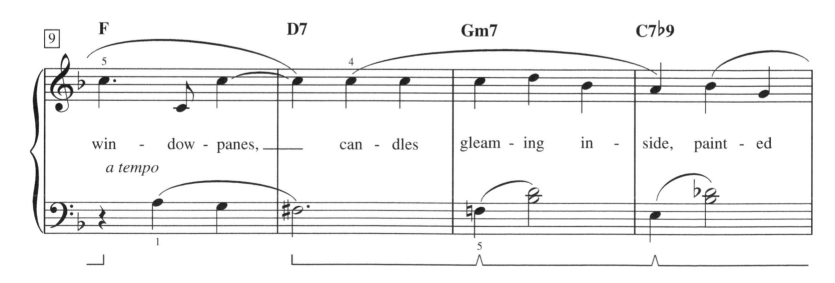

20

21

I'LL BE HOME FOR CHRISTMAS

Words and Music by KIM GANNON
and WALTER KENT
Arranged by Phillip Keveren

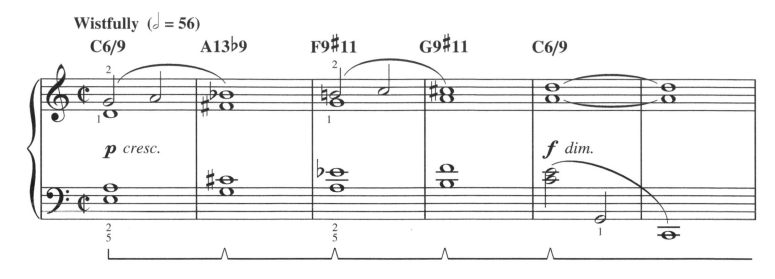

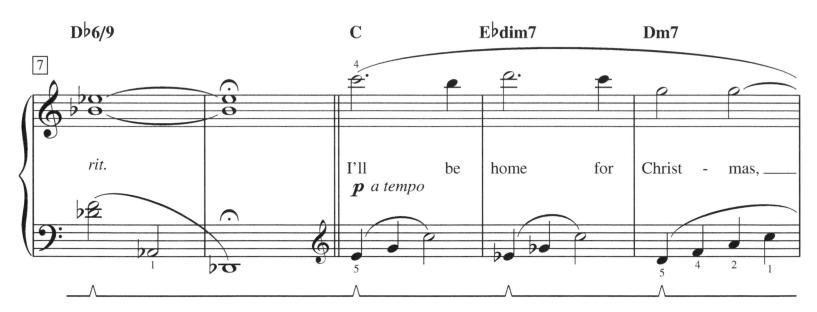

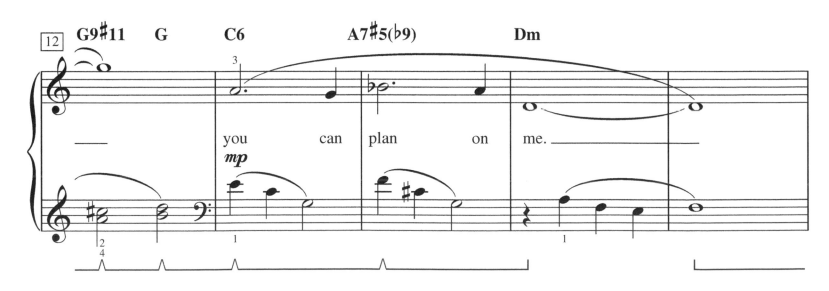

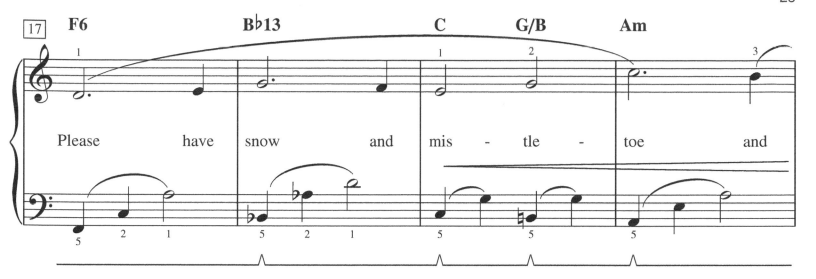

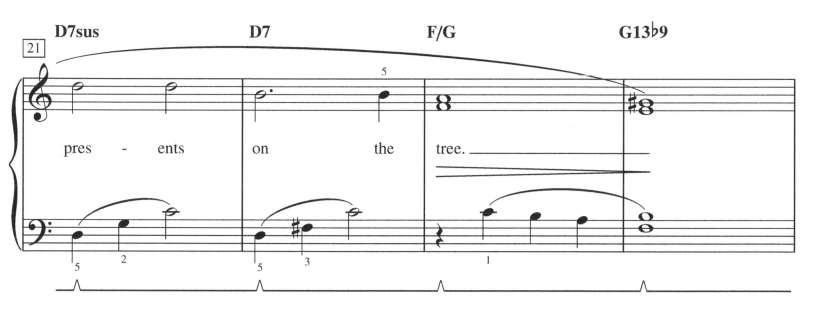

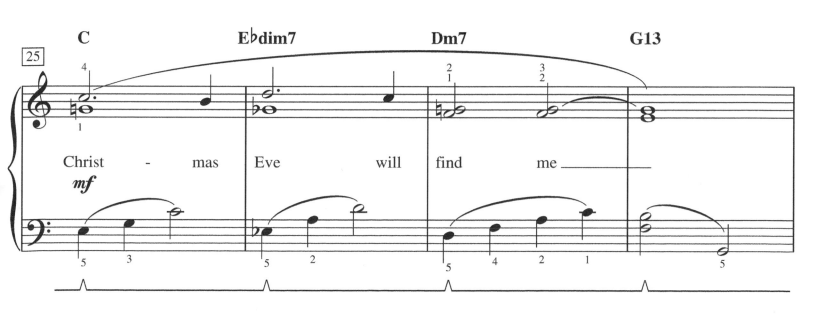

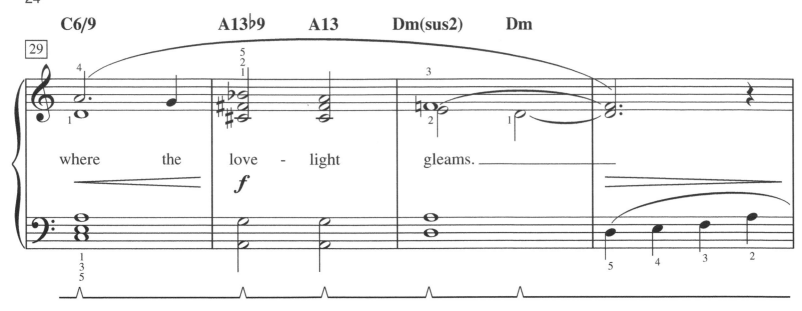

where the love - light gleams.

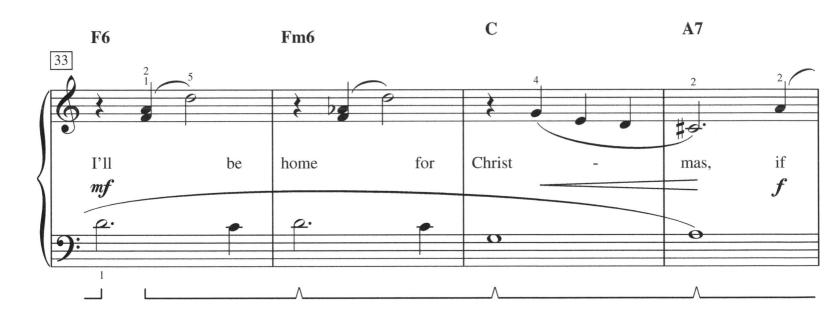

I'll be home for Christ - mas, if

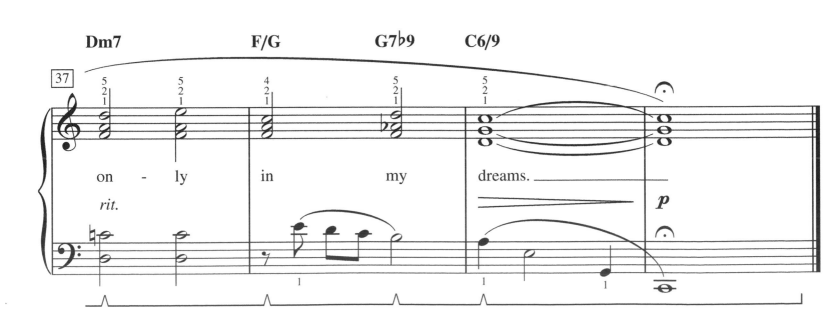

on - ly in my dreams.

RUDOLPH, THE RED-NOSED REINDEER

Music and Lyrics by
JOHNNY MARKS
Arranged by Phillip Keveren

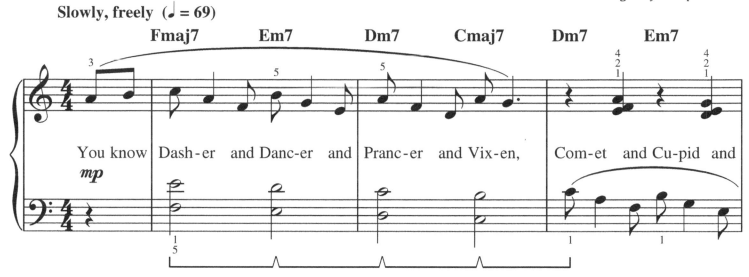

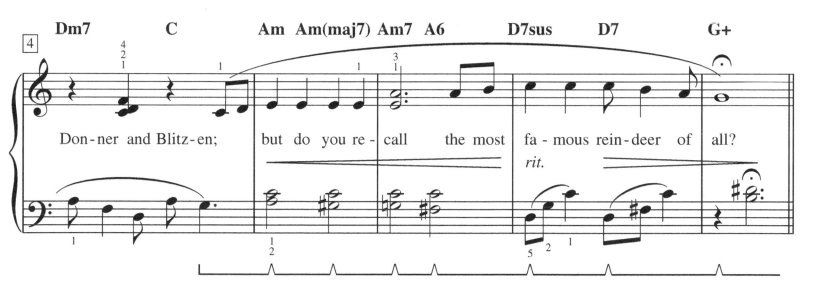

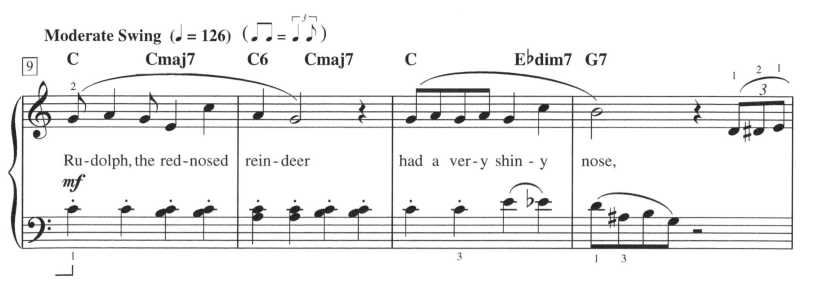

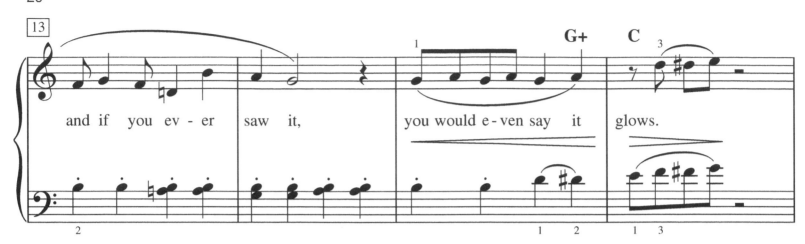

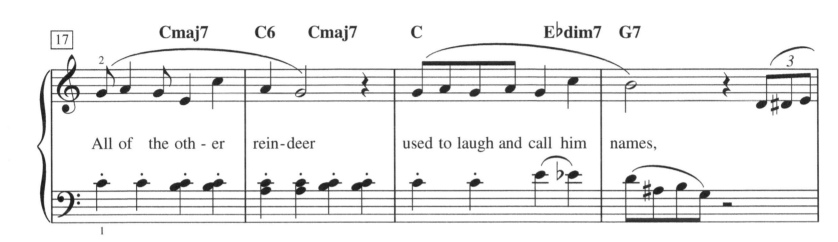

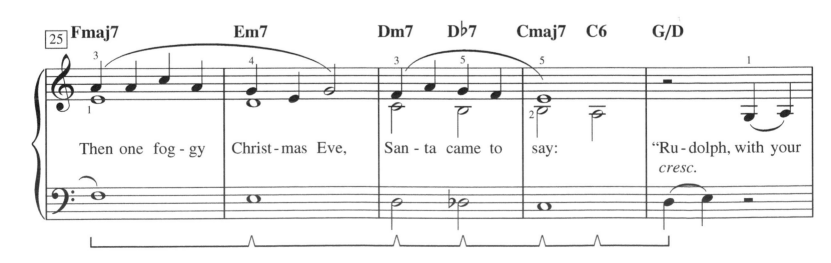

nose so bright, won't you guide my sleigh to-night?"

Then how the rein-deer loved him as they shout-ed out with

glee: "Ru-dolph, the red-nosed rein-deer, you'll go down in

his - to - ry!"

JINGLE BELLS

Words and Music by
J. PIERPONT
Arranged by Phillip Keveren

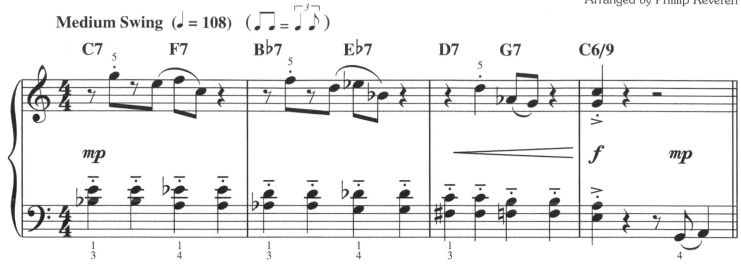

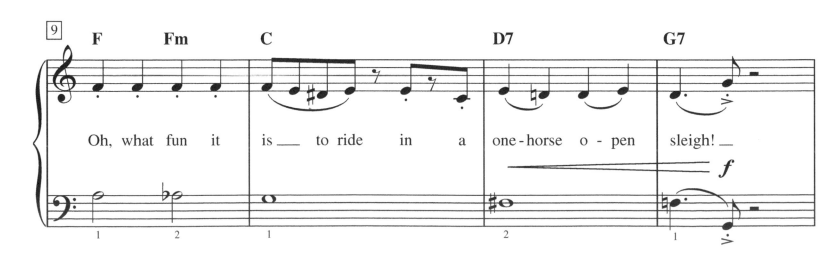

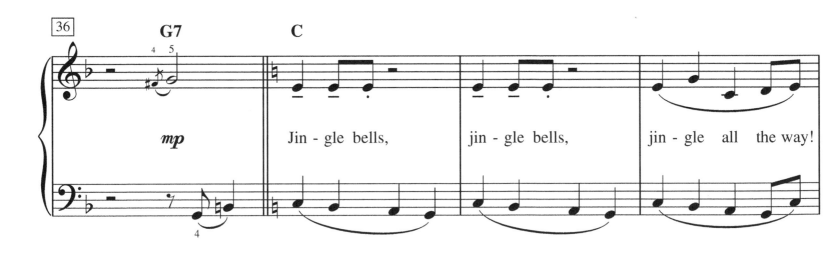

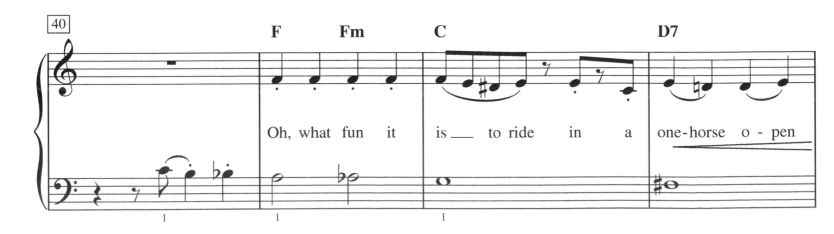

sleigh! — Jin - gle bells, jin - gle bells, jin - gle all the way!

Oh, what fun it is ___ to ride in a

one - horse o - pen, one - horse o - pen sleigh!

LET IT SNOW! LET IT SNOW! LET IT SNOW!

Words by SAMMY CAHN
Music by JULE STYNE
Arranged by Phillip Keveren

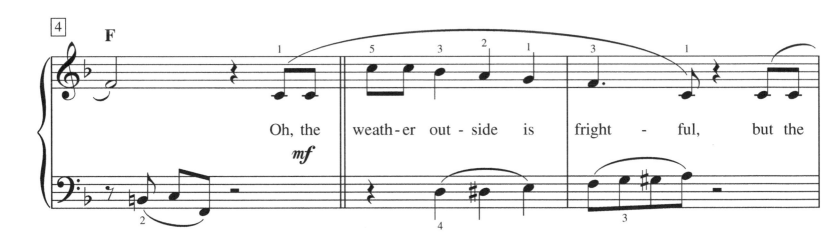

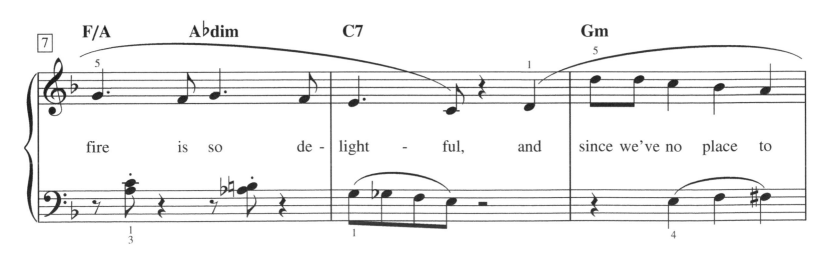

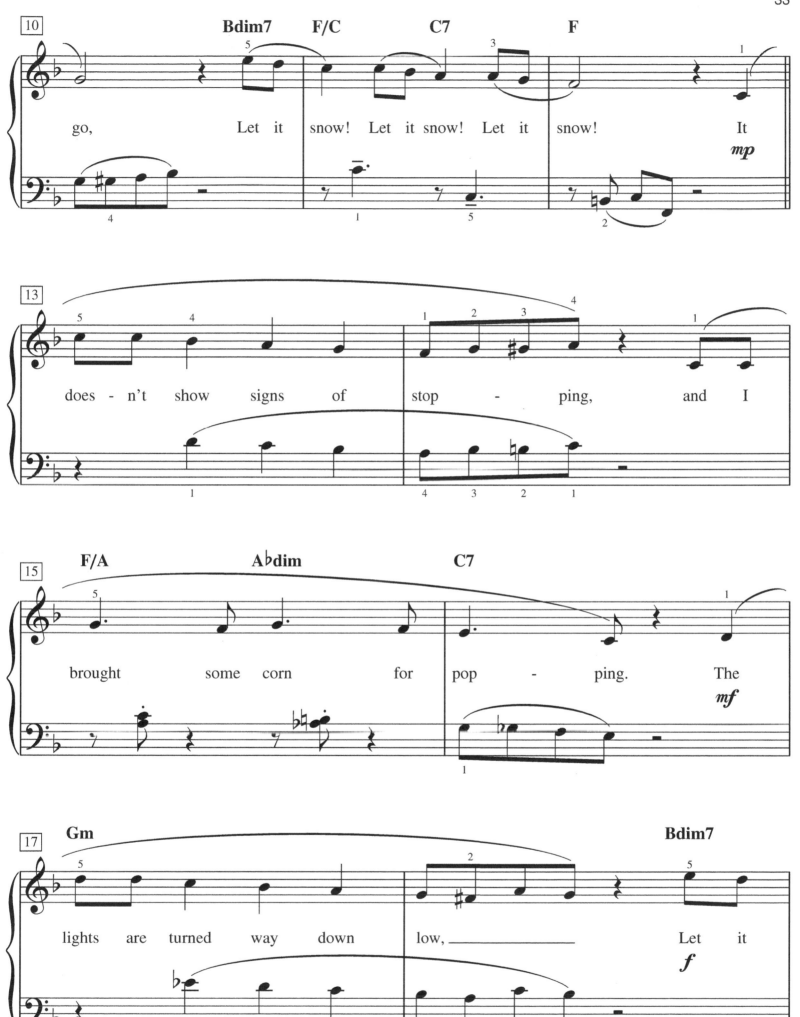

34

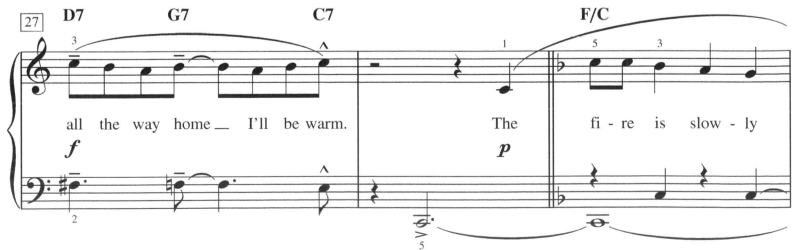

THE MOST WONDERFUL TIME OF THE YEAR

Words and Music by EDDIE POLA
and GEORGE WYLE
Arranged by Phillip Keveren

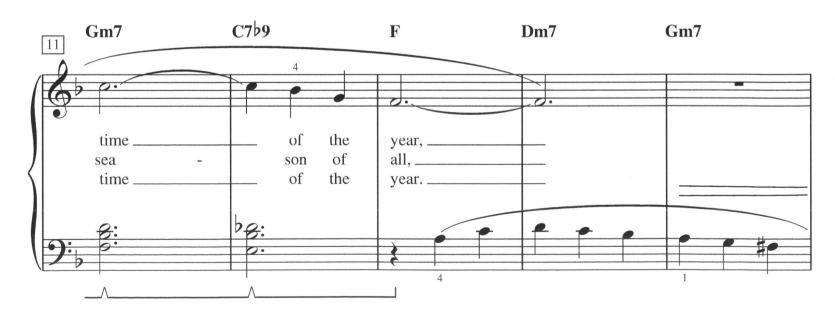

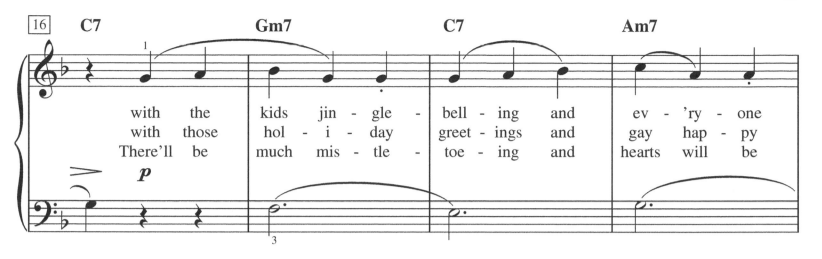

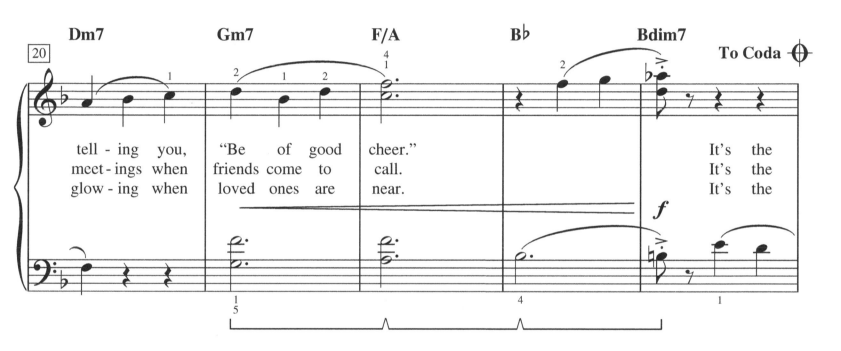

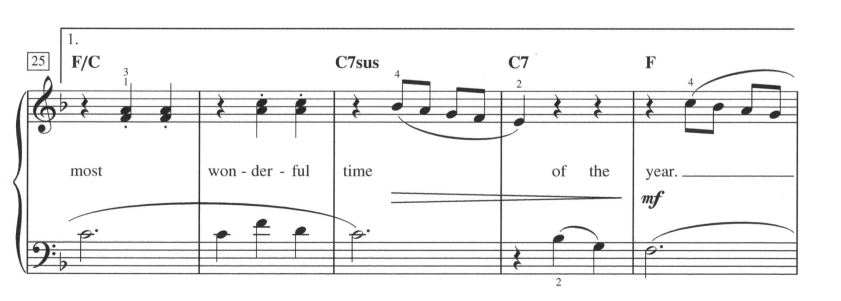

38

39

SANTA CLAUS IS COMIN' TO TOWN

Words by HAVEN GILLESPIE
Music by J. FRED COOTS
Arranged by Phillip Keveren

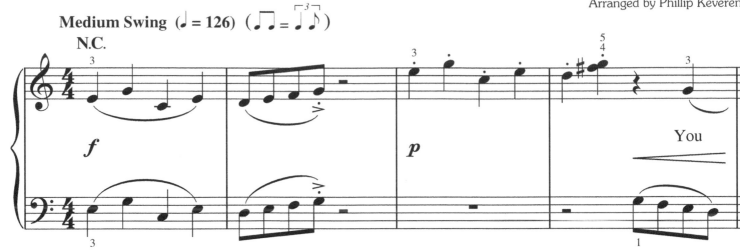

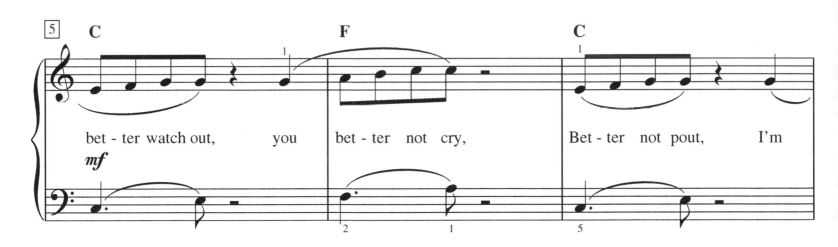

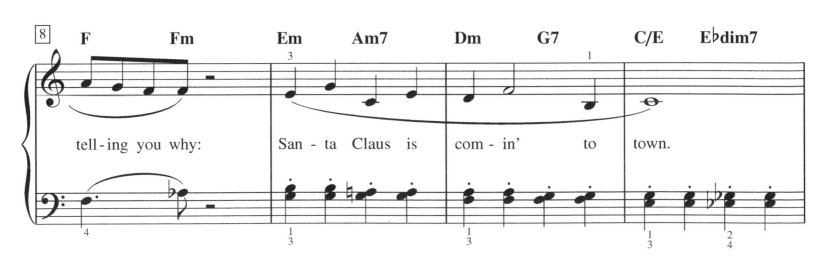

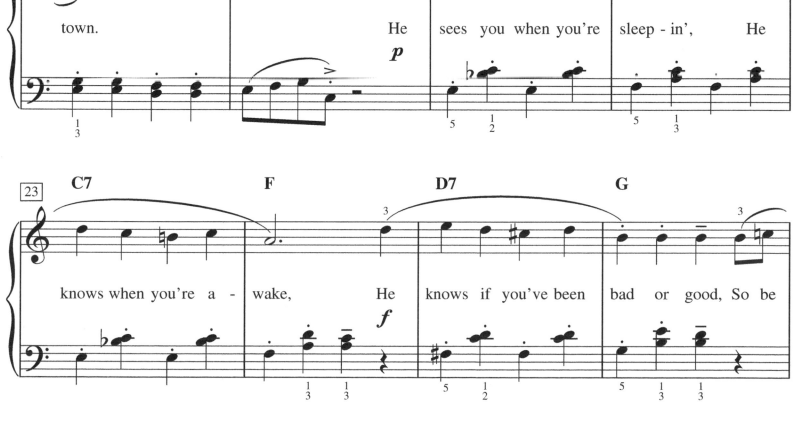

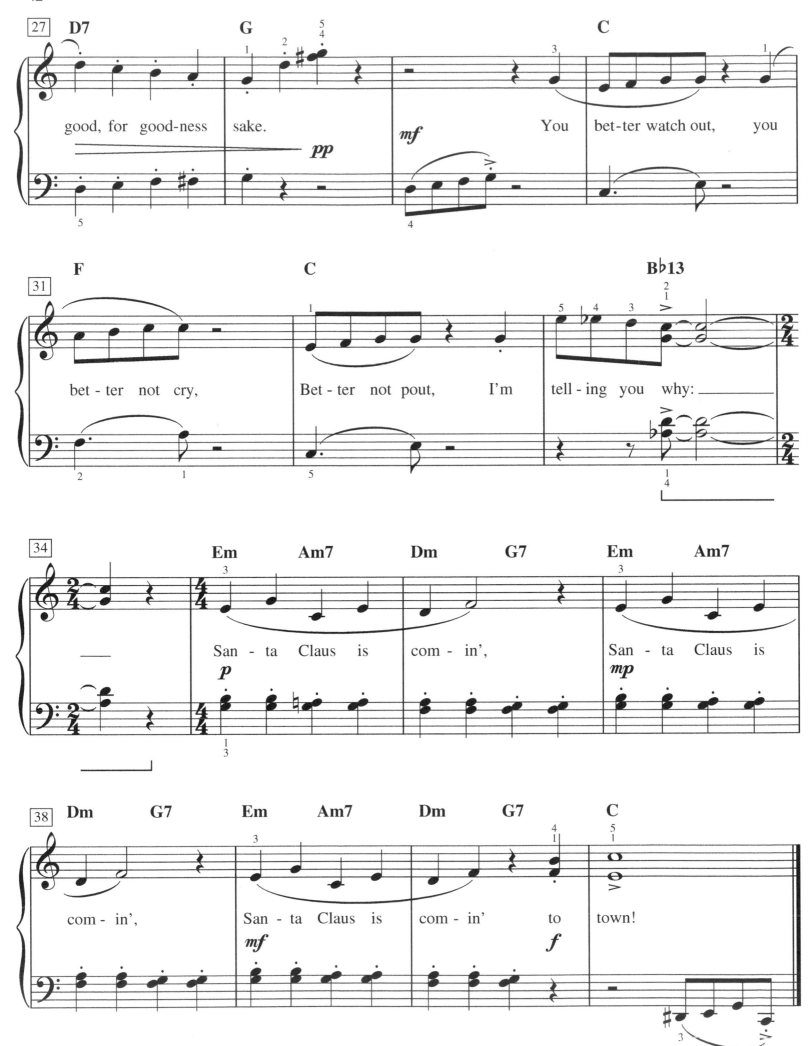

SILVER BELLS
from the Paramount Picture THE LEMON DROP KID

Words and Music by JAY LIVINGSTON
and RAY EVANS
Arranged by Phillip Keveren

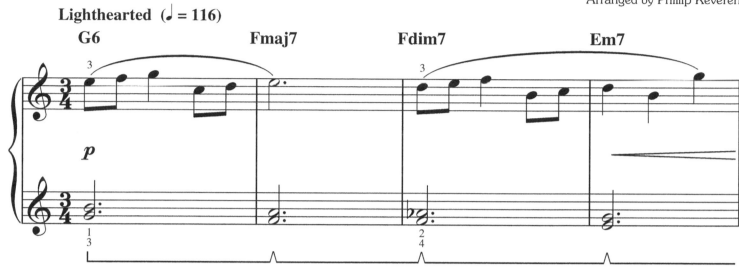

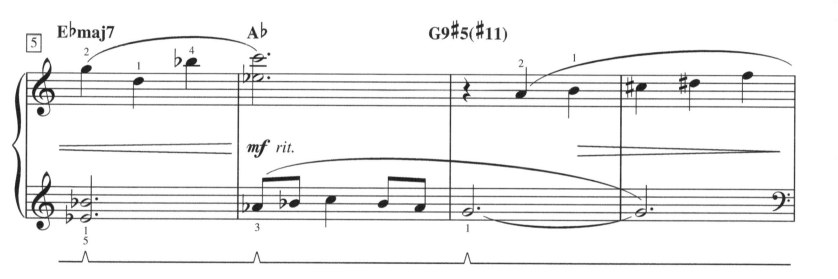

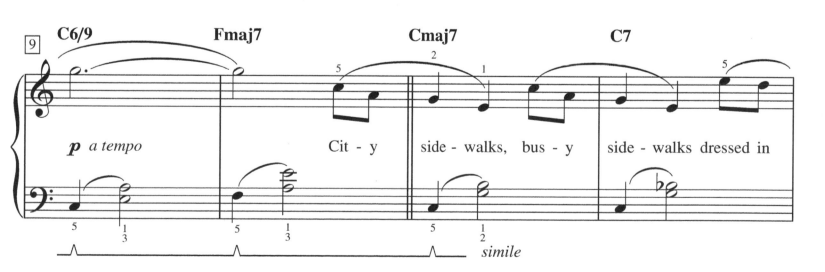

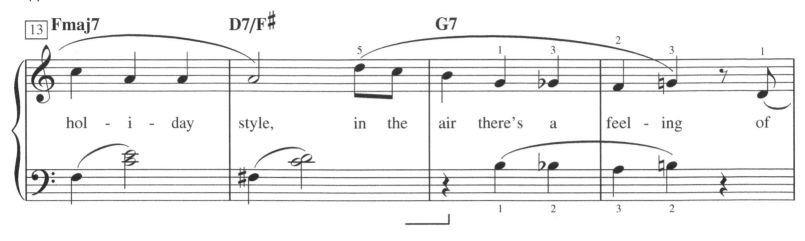

13 **Fmaj7**   **D7/F♯**   **G7**

hol - i - day   style,   in the   air   there's   a   feel - ing   of

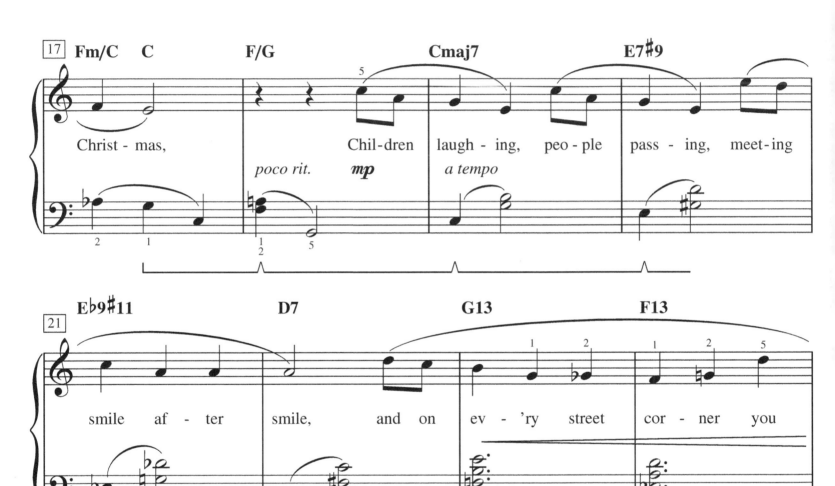

17 **Fm/C** **C**   **F/G**   **Cmaj7**   **E7♯9**

Christ - mas,   Chil-dren   laugh - ing,   peo - ple   pass - ing,   meet-ing

poco rit.   *mp*   *a tempo*

21 **E♭9♯11**   **D7**   **G13**   **F13**

smile af - ter   smile,   and on   ev - 'ry   street   cor - ner   you

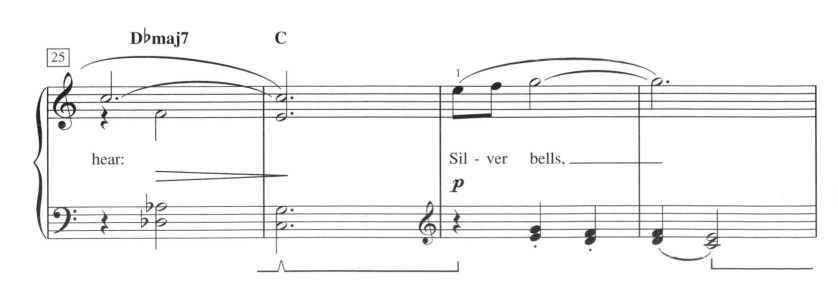

25 **D♭maj7**   **C**

hear: Sil - ver bells,_____

p

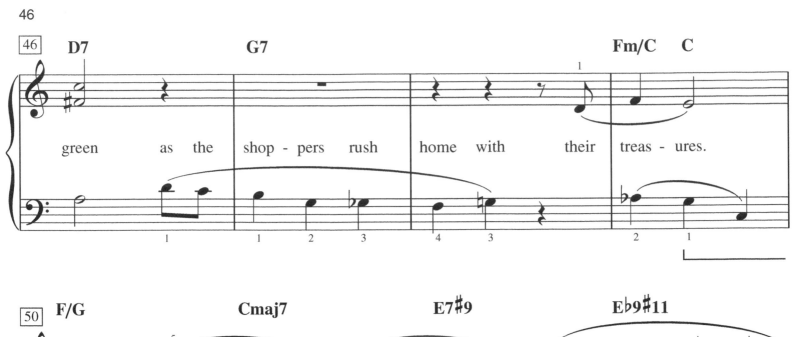

green   as the   shop - pers rush   home with   their   treas - ures.

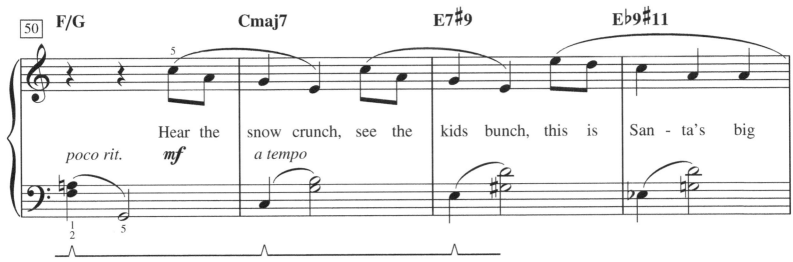

poco rit. **mf** *a tempo*

Hear the   snow crunch, see the   kids bunch, this is   San - ta's   big

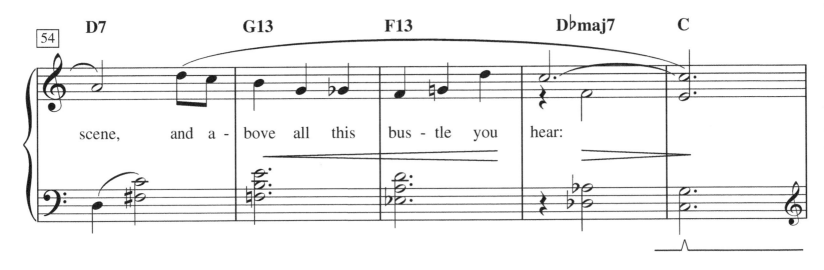

scene,   and a - bove all this   bus - tle you   hear:

Sil - ver bells, _____   sil - ver bells, _____

p

SKATING

By VINCE GUARALDI
Arranged by Phillip Keveren

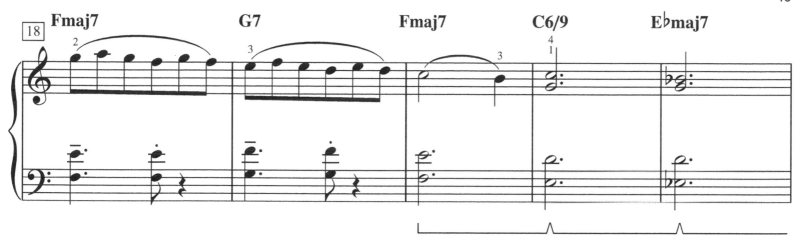

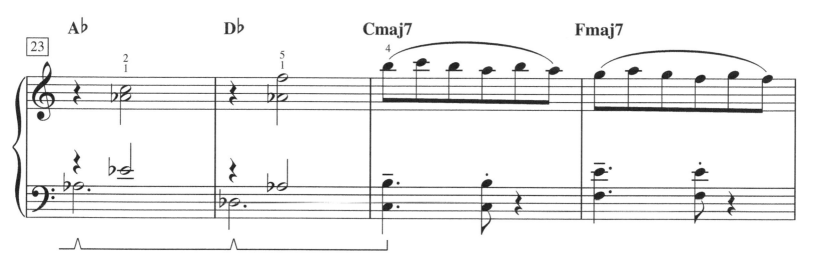

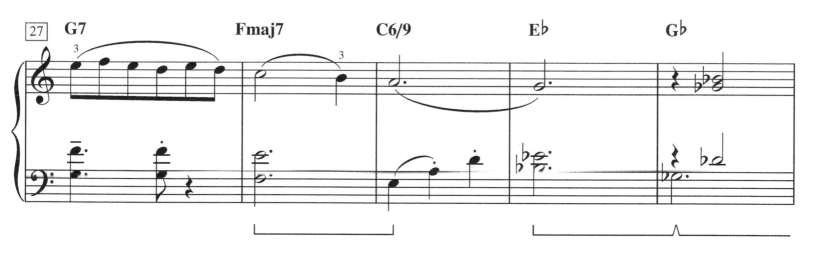

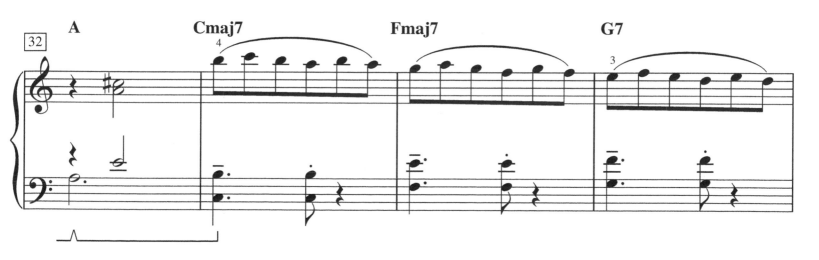

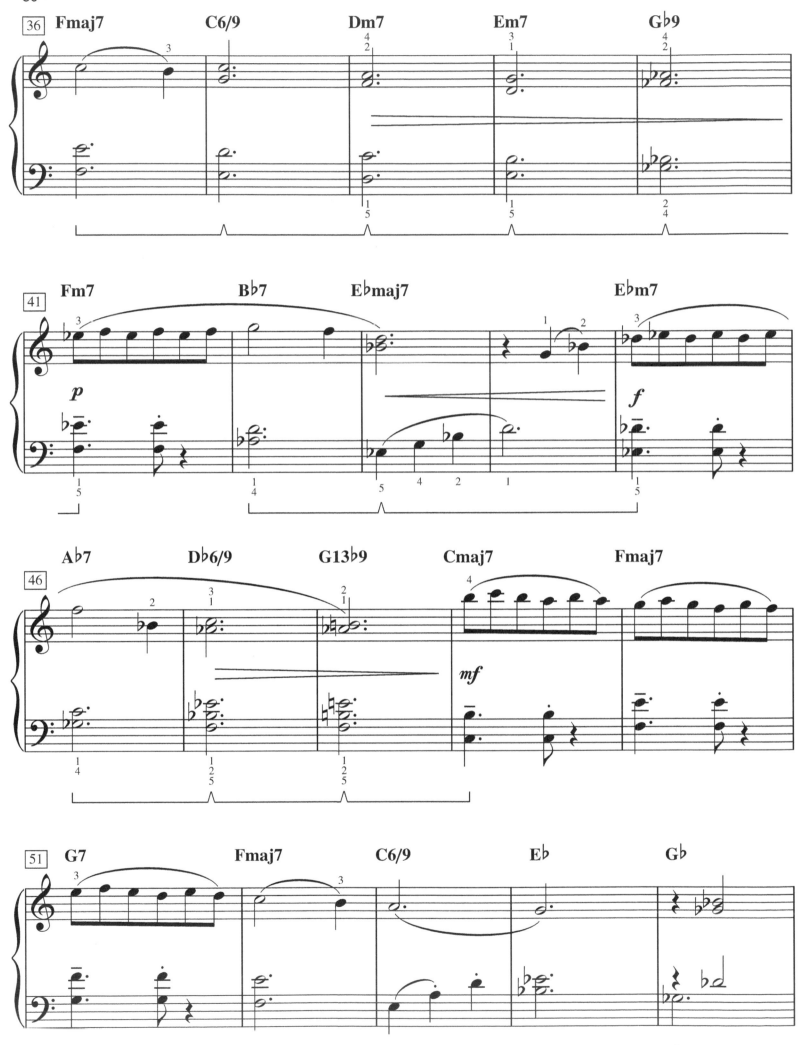

UP ON THE HOUSETOP

Words and Music by
B.R. HANBY
Arranged by Phillip Keveren

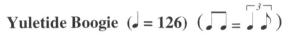

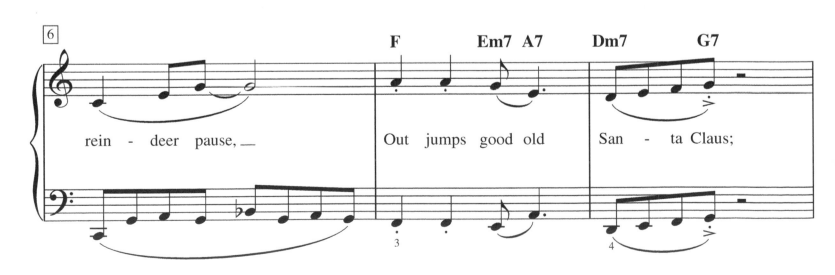

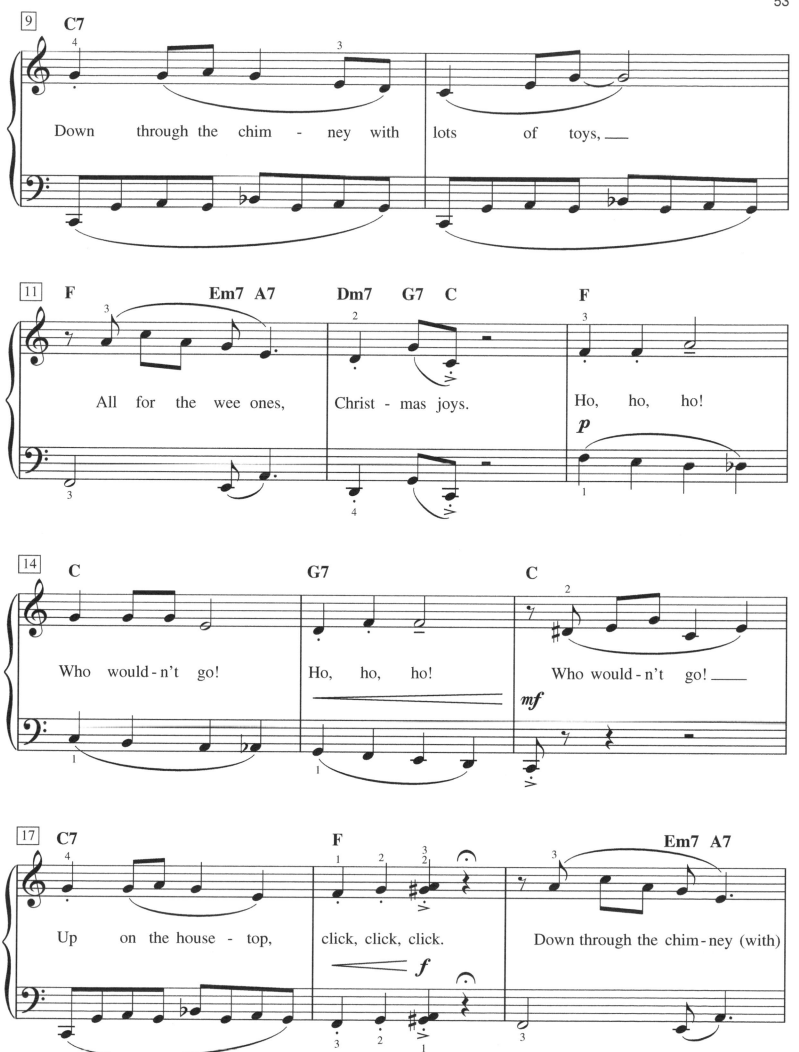

WE WISH YOU A MERRY CHRISTMAS

Traditional English Folksong
Arranged by Phillip Keveren

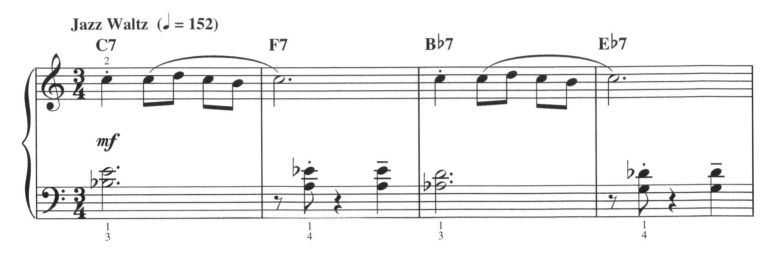

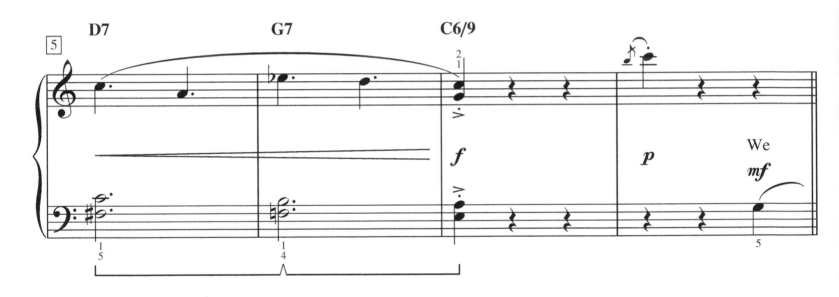

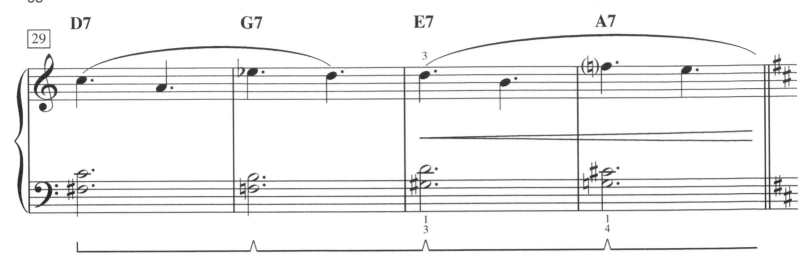

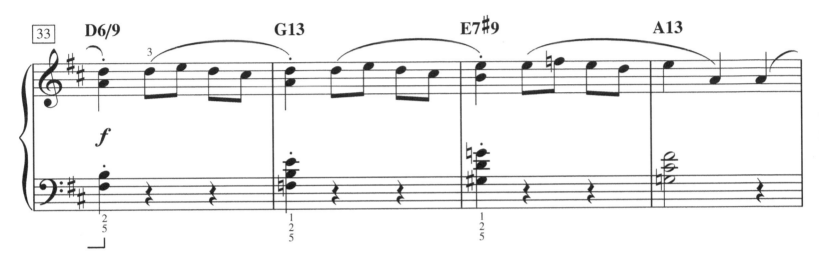

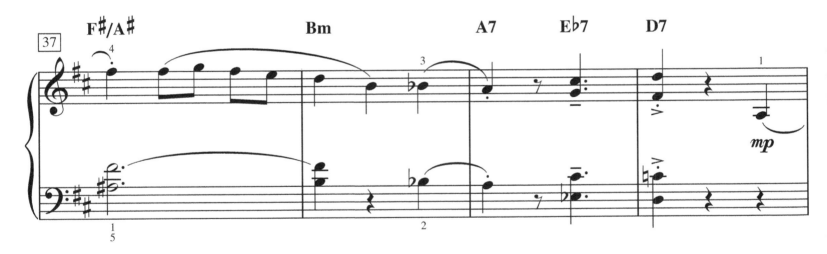

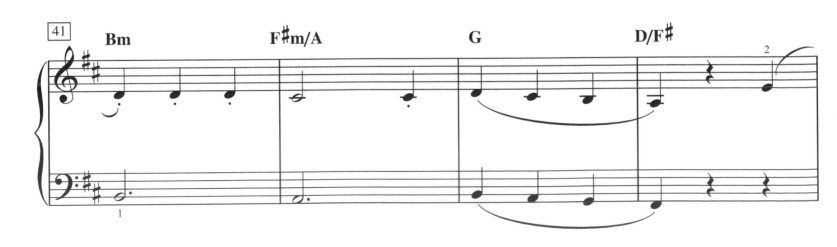

SNOWFALL

Lyrics by RUTH THORNHILL
Music by CLAUDE THORNHILL
Arranged by Phillip Keveren

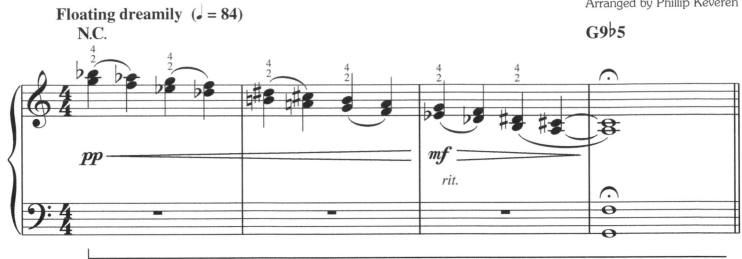

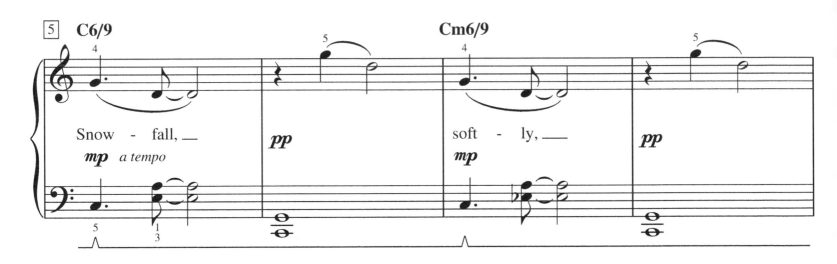

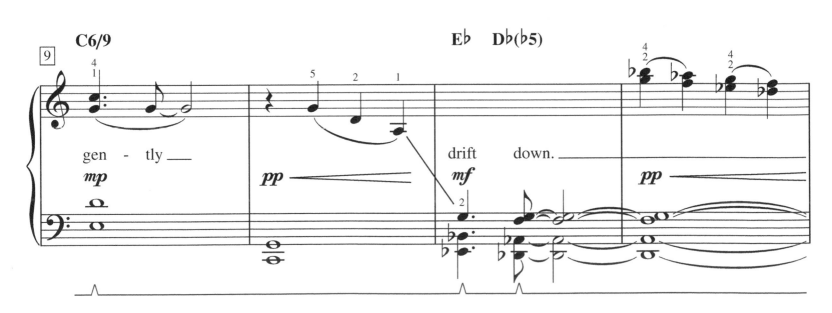

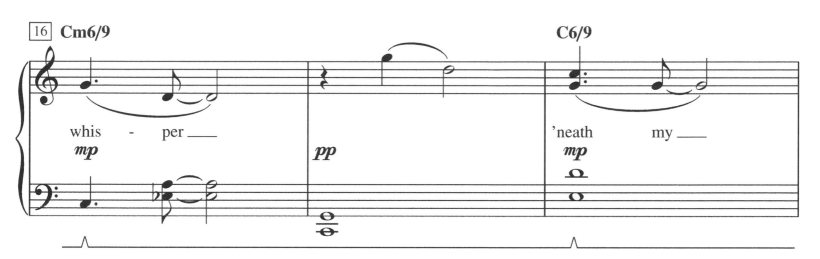

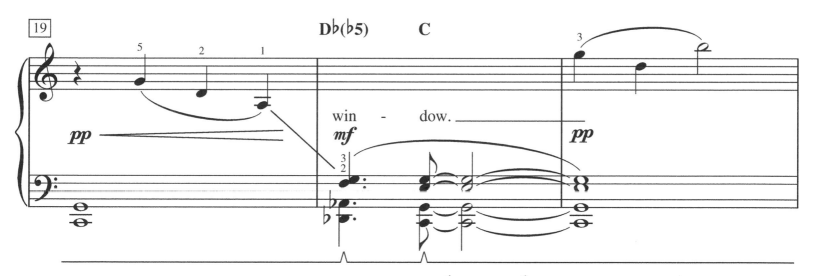

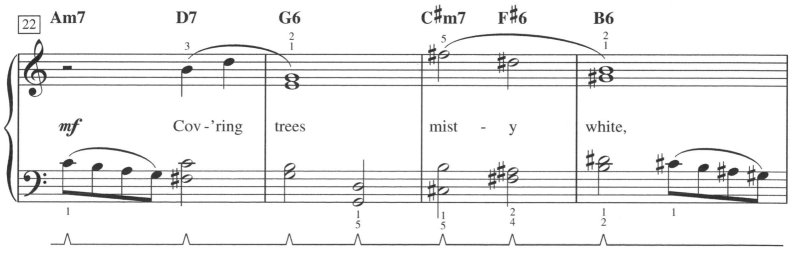

62

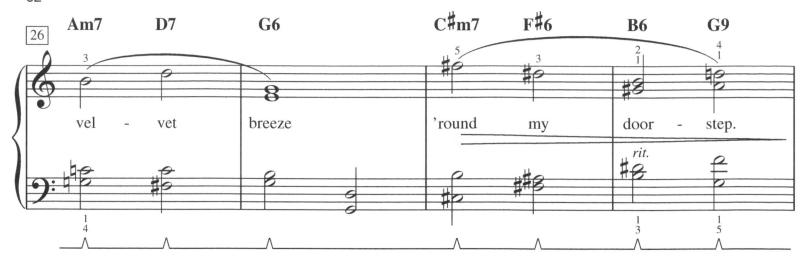

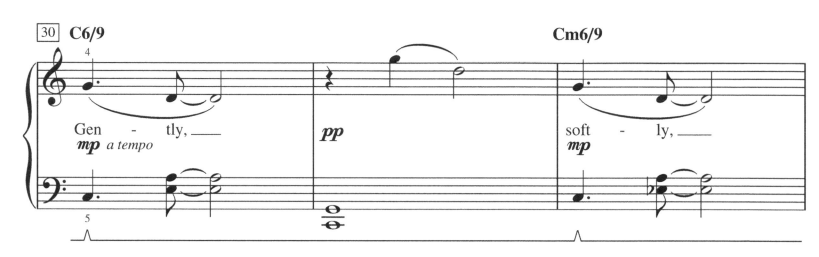

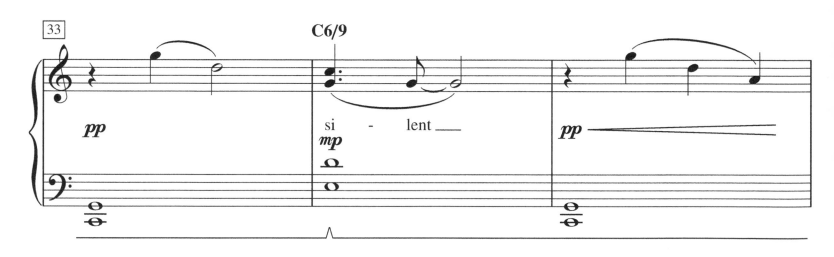

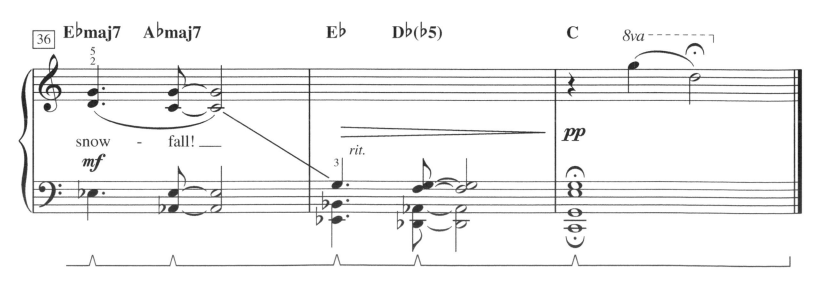

THE PHILLIP KEVEREN SERIES

PIANO SOLO

00156644	**ABBA for Classical Piano**	$15.99
00311024	**Above All**	$12.99
00311348	**Americana**	$12.99
00198473	**Bach Meets Jazz**	$14.99
00313594	**Bacharach and David**	$15.99
00306412	**The Beatles**	$17.99
00312189	**The Beatles for Classical Piano**	$16.99
00275876	**The Beatles – Recital Suites**	$19.99
00312546	**Best Piano Solos**	$15.99
00156601	**Blessings**	$12.99
00198656	**Blues Classics**	$12.99
00284359	**Broadway Songs with a Classical Flair**	$14.99
00310669	**Broadway's Best**	$14.99
00312106	**Canzone Italiana**	$12.99
00280848	**Carpenters**	$16.99
00310629	**A Celtic Christmas**	$12.99
00310549	**The Celtic Collection**	$12.95
00280571	**Celtic Songs with a Classical Flair**	$12.99
00263362	**Charlie Brown Favorites**	$14.99
00312190	**Christmas at the Movies**	$14.99
00294754	**Christmas Carols with a Classical Flair**	$12.99
00311414	**Christmas Medleys**	$14.99
00236669	**Christmas Praise Hymns**	$12.99
00233788	**Christmas Songs for Classical Piano**	$12.99
00311769	**Christmas Worship Medleys**	$14.99
00310607	**Cinema Classics**	$15.99
00301857	**Circles**	$10.99
00311101	**Classic Wedding Songs**	$10.95
00311292	**Classical Folk**	$10.95
00311083	**Classical Jazz**	$12.95
00137779	**Coldplay for Classical Piano**	$16.99
00311103	**Contemporary Wedding Songs**	$12.99
00348788	**Country Songs with a Classical Flair**	$14.99
00249097	**Disney Recital Suites**	$17.99
00311754	**Disney Songs for Classical Piano**	$17.99
00241379	**Disney Songs for Ragtime Piano**	$17.99
00311881	**Favorite Wedding Songs**	$14.99
00315974	**Fiddlin' at the Piano**	$12.99
00311811	**The Film Score Collection**	$15.99
00269408	**Folksongs with a Classical Flair**	$12.99
00144353	**The Gershwin Collection**	$14.99
00233789	**Golden Scores**	$14.99
00144351	**Gospel Greats**	$12.99
00183566	**The Great American Songbook**	$12.99
00312084	**The Great Melodies**	$12.99
00311157	**Great Standards**	$12.95
00171621	**A Grown-Up Christmas List**	$12.99
00311071	**The Hymn Collection**	$12.99
00311349	**Hymn Medleys**	$12.99

00280705	**Hymns in a Celtic Style**	$12.99
00269407	**Hymns with a Classical Flair**	$12.99
00311249	**Hymns with a Touch of Jazz**	$12.99
00310905	**I Could Sing of Your Love Forever**	$12.95
00310762	**Jingle Jazz**	$14.99
00175310	**Billy Joel for Classical Piano**	$16.99
00126449	**Elton John for Classical Piano**	$16.99
00310839	**Let Freedom Ring!**	$12.99
00238988	**Andrew Lloyd Webber Piano Songbook**	$14.99
00313227	**Andrew Lloyd Webber Solos**	$15.99
00313523	**Mancini Magic**	$16.99
00312113	**More Disney Songs for Classical Piano**	$16.99
00311295	**Motown Hits**	$14.99
00300640	**Piano Calm**	$12.99
00339131	**Piano Calm: Christmas**	$12.99
00346009	**Piano Calm: Prayer**	$14.99
00306870	**Piazzolla Tangos**	$16.99
00156645	**Queen for Classical Piano**	$15.99
00310755	**Richard Rodgers Classics**	$16.99
00289545	**Scottish Songs**	$12.99
00310609	**Shout to the Lord!**	$14.99
00119403	**The Sound of Music**	$14.99
00311978	**The Spirituals Collection**	$10.99
00210445	**Star Wars**	$16.99
00224738	**Symphonic Hymns for Piano**	$14.99
00279673	**Tin Pan Alley**	$12.99
00312112	**Treasured Hymns for Classical Piano**	$14.99
00144926	**The Twelve Keys of Christmas**	$12.99
00278486	**The Who for Classical Piano**	$16.99
00294036	**Worship with a Touch of Jazz**	$12.99
00311911	**Yuletide Jazz**	$17.99

EASY PIANO

00210401	**Adele for Easy Classical Piano**	$15.99
00310610	**African-American Spirituals**	$10.99
00218244	**The Beatles for Easy Classical Piano**	$14.99
00218387	**Catchy Songs for Piano**	$12.99
00310973	**Celtic Dreams**	$12.99
00233686	**Christmas Carols for Easy Classical Piano**	$12.99
00311126	**Christmas Pops**	$14.99
00311548	**Classic Pop/Rock Hits**	$14.99
00310769	**A Classical Christmas**	$10.95
00310975	**Classical Movie Themes**	$12.99
00144352	**Disney Songs for Easy Classical Piano**	$12.99
00311093	**Early Rock 'n' Roll**	$14.99
00311997	**Easy Worship Medleys**	$12.99
00289547	**Duke Ellington**	$14.99
00160297	**Folksongs for Easy Classical Piano**	$12.99

00110374	**George Gershwin Classics**	$12.99
00310805	**Gospel Treasures**	$12.99
00306821	**Vince Guaraldi Collection**	$19.99
00160294	**Hymns for Easy Classical Piano**	$12.99
00310798	**Immortal Hymns**	$12.99
00311294	**Jazz Standards**	$12.99
00310744	**Love Songs**	$12.99
00233740	**The Most Beautiful Songs for Easy Classical Piano**	$12.99
00220036	**Pop Ballads**	$14.99
00311406	**Pop Gems of the 1950s**	$12.95
00311407	**Pop Gems of the 1960s**	$12.95
00233739	**Pop Standards for Easy Classical Piano**	$12.99
00102887	**A Ragtime Christmas**	$12.99
00311293	**Ragtime Classics**	$10.95
00312028	**Santa Swings**	$12.99
00233688	**Songs from Childhood for Easy Classical Piano**	$12.99
00103258	**Songs of Inspiration**	$12.99
00310840	**Sweet Land of Liberty**	$12.99
00126450	**10,000 Reasons**	$14.99
00310712	**Timeless Praise**	$12.95
00311086	**TV Themes**	$12.99
00310717	**21 Great Classics**	$12.99
00160076	**Waltzes & Polkas for Easy Classical Piano**	$12.99
00145342	**Weekly Worship**	$16.99

BIG-NOTE PIANO

00310838	**Children's Favorite Movie Songs**	$12.99
00346000	**Christmas Movie Magic**	$12.99
00277368	**Classical Favorites**	$12.99
00310907	**Contemporary Hits**	$12.99
00277370	**Disney Favorites**	$14.99
00310888	**Joy to the World**	$12.99
00310908	**The Nutcracker**	$12.99
00277371	**Star Wars**	$16.99

BEGINNING PIANO SOLOS

00311202	**Awesome God**	$12.99
00310837	**Christian Children's Favorites**	$12.99
00311117	**Christmas Traditions**	$10.99
00311250	**Easy Hymns**	$12.99
00102710	**Everlasting God**	$10.99
00311403	**Jazzy Tunes**	$10.95
00310822	**Kids' Favorites**	$12.99
00338175	**Silly Songs for Kids**	$9.99

PIANO DUET

00126452	**The Christmas Variations**	$12.99
00311350	**Classical Theme Duets**	$10.99
00295099	**Gospel Duets**	$12.99
00311544	**Hymn Duets**	$14.99
00311203	**Praise & Worship Duets**	$12.99
00294755	**Sacred Christmas Duets**	$12.99
00119405	**Star Wars**	$14.99
00253545	**Worship Songs for Two**	$12.99

Hal•Leonard®

Search songlists, more products and place your order from your favorite music retailer at
halleonard.com

Prices, contents, and availability subject to change without notice.

0221

158

0117